BOOKS BY OGDEN NASH

THE OLD DOG
BARKS BACKWARDS

THE OLD DOG
BARKS BACKWARDS

by

OGDEN NASH

Illustrated by

ROBERT BINKS

LITTLE, BROWN AND COMPANY — BOSTON–TORONTO

Many of these poems first appeared in magazines and are reprinted
through the courtesy of the following: *ASCAP Today, Atlantic Monthly,
Boys' Life, Clipper, Ford Times, Gourmet, Holiday, Horizon, Look,
McCall's, The New Yorker, Odyssey, Saturday Review, Signature, Travel
& Camera*, and *Venture*.

Library of Congress Cataloging in Publication Data

Nash, Ogden, 1902-1971.
    The old dog barks backwards.

    Poems.
    I. Title.
PS3527.A637O4 1972   811'.5'2   76-186967
ISBN 0-316-59804-6

*Published simultaneously in Canada
by Little, Brown & Company (Canada) Limited*

CONTENTS

THE OLD DOG
BARKS BACKWARDS

AND LO!
HONORÉ'S NAME
LED ALL THE REST

Myself when young was prone to conform to youthful
　　mores;
Consequently, my acquaintance with Balzac was lim-
　　ited to his opus best adapted to youthful tastes,
　　"Droll Stories."
Yet even then I understood that as a novelist he was
　　undoubtedly major,
And I vowed that to read his complete works would
　　be my project when I should matriculate at some
　　Sunset Haven as a retiree and Golden Ager,
Because, to be truly cultured, a person should read the
　　complete works of at least one major man of letters,
　　or so they say,
And I decided that on my literary menu Balzac should
　　be the *spécialité*.
I planned to devote each weekend from *Vendredi*
　　through *Samedi* to "The Human Comedy";
I looked forward with a wild surmise
To meeting "Cousin Bette" and "Cousin Pons," to say
　　nothing of "The Girl with the Golden Eyes";
Also, if only to discover what its title denotes,
"The House of the Cat Who Pelotes."

[3]

I should then have absorbed all Balzac, there could be
no more.
But now I suddenly find that besides Honoré de there
was another Balzac: Seigneur Jean Louis Guez
(gâz) de, 1597(?)–1654,
And that praise for his prose was once on every literate
lip,
Chiefly because he wrote "The Barbon" and "The
Aristippe."
That's too many Balzacs for one gray head; I shall turn
instead to the plays of Sir William Davenant,
And should you ask me if I have read anything by
either Balzac other than "Droll Stories," well, I
havenant.

FOR RUDOLF FRIML
ON HIS NINETIETH BIRTHDAY

Deep in the social archives let us delve
For what's been going on since 1912
When Teddy Roosevelt boomed his Bull Moose cry
And Emma Trentini graced *The Firefly*.
Ye who to life today confess an allergy,
Come join me in a spell of mild nostalagy;
Think what we've lost, think what we've gained
    instead;
I fear the audit finds us in the red.
Long, long before Lombardo, Rudolf Friml
Gave us the sweetest music this side of *Himmel*;
Now adolescing tycoons our eardrums doom
With sound as shattering as a sonic boom.
The Hesitation Waltz, the Castle Walk
Have vanished with Dorothy Arnold and the auk;
Now dance floors crack neath measures less exquisite,
From Twist to Frug to Watusi to Watisit.
How childish to the modern ear and eye
The catchwords of an ingenuous age gone by!
Lothario with gaudy-ribboned lid
Whispered, "I love my wife, but oh you kid!"
Or, were he bold as all get-out, or Hades,
"You tell 'em, corset, you been around the ladies!"
And if the pretty fish refused to nibble,

[6]

Departed with a jaunty "Ish Kabibble!"
Today should maid perchance eschew his bed
(Fat chance!), he'd snarl a chivalrous "Drop dead!"
The press, not TV, was the nation's voice;
Twixt tenor, bass, soprano, you had your choice.
At morning with their banners wide unfurled,
Tribune, American, Herald and the *World,*
And for the later news a man could probe
Sun, Telegram, Mail, Journal and the *Globe*
And still fall victim to the talents huckstery
Of Horatio Alger urchins shouting, "Wuxtry!"
All, all are gone, the old familiar mastheads,
Torn down by Munsey, Powers and such-like bast
    heads.

How self-respecting matrons raised their brows
At sight of hussy in a peekaboo blouse;
Their great-granddaughters now with face cherubic
Flaunt skirts which some call mini, I call pubic.
In 1912 bad boys in blue serge knickers
Read *Cap'n Billy's Whizzbang* for their snickers,
'Twas the sole sex-oriented school for lads
Except the gutter and the corset ads;
Even in the 20's we lacked a proper schooling;
We thought Savoy and Brennan were only fooling,
While kindergarteners in today's America
Write in for curiosa and esoterica,
And daily indulge, 'twixt pot and peanut butter,
In practices unheard of in the gutter.
Old Seneca watched the rotting Roman banners

And mourned, "What once were vices now are man-
ners."
Today romance is jeered and science our tutor,
The goddess moon now manifestly neuter.
Yet, from a sweeter age that used to be
Comes the melody to ease our malady.
The Friml magic stirs the turgid air
And eases our frustration and despair.
I trust that your conclusion and mine are similar:
'Twould be a happier world if it were Frimler.

AT LEAST I'M NOT
THE KIND OF FOOL
WHO SOBS,
WHAT KIND OF FOOL AM I?

Since April is the foolest month I shall make the most
  of it,
Sit at the Captain's table on the Ship of Fools and be
  the toast of it.
I shall pronounce with profundity
Judgments solemn and pundity,
Steal quotations from Bartlett's
To impress nymphets and tartlets,
And interpret Kafka
To the rifka and rafka.
I shall let it be known that I know Elia was really
  Charles Lamb and Voltaire was really Arouet,
And I shall appear as regularly as Phyllis Diller with
  Mike Douglas, Merv Griffin, Johnny Carson, David
  or Dave Frost and Dave or David Garroway.
Should I meet an ambishop young clergyman anxious
  for a diocese
I shall warn him against the occupational disease of
  preachers and politicians, eloquentiasis.
Should I meet Miss Streisand I shall reach into my
  hat with a cry of Abracadabra
And restore to her the *a* missing from Barbra.

I shall matriculate at the Pentagon for a course in military-industrial complexes, and if I flunk,
I shall debouch into a debauch in Mauch Chunk.
I shall speak to the Administration like a kindly old brother
And console it with the assurance that if it loses this war it can always find another.
At this point my foolish bubble may be bursted,
But in the pursuit of folly I refuse to be bested or worsted.

BET YOU A NICKEL MY UNHAPPINESS CAN LICK YOUR UNHAPPINESS

The world is full of bath towels and cocktail glasses
   and washrooms marked Hers and His,
And even fuller of darling little aphorisms and apo-
   phthegms beginning Happiness is.
Perhaps my sense of whimsy has withered, has shriv-
   eled, is wizened,
But I think it's time to take a look at unhappiness,
   which is what happiness isn't.
Unhappiness is having aisle seats in the theatre and
   people stumble over your feet with or without an
   apologetic smile;
It is also having seats in the center of the row and
   you stumble over the feet of people sitting on the
   aisle.
Unhappiness is being trapped on a rainy highway
   with a slow-moving truck in front of you and a
   fast-moving truck coming up behind you.
Unhappiness is forgetting what it was of which you
   had meant to remind your wife to remind you.
It is a female teen-ager in the family whose very
   ideal is Raquel Welch or Faye Dunaway;
It is the corner of the rug that keeps curling up and

it is the three-way light bulb that works only one-
away.
It is when you finally manage to fit both your check
and that computer-slotted slat into the envelope
with the window slit provided by your utility cartel,
and it is at best an awkward fit,
And you stamp it and seal it only to find that you have
to rip it open again because the wrong side of the
slotted slat is facing the slit.
Yes, the world is truly full of a number of things.
No wonder we are all usually as unhappy as kings.

BEWARE OF
EASTER MONDAY

Comes a feast day and I am a fair to middling feaster,
I even go so far as to finish off the cloves in the ham at
Easter.
My plate is clean enough to be eaten off by Amy Van-
derbilt or Mrs. Grundy;
But what about Easter Monday?
On Thanksgiving, naturally, it's turkey and cranberry,
This you can count on from coast to coast, from
Seattle to Danbury.
The same at Christmas, though somewhat more in-
digestible,
Because of that seasonal additive, plum pudding, the
popular combustible comestible.
Nevertheless, a pretty dish to set before a queen, as
Catherine de Médicis remarked to the Prince de
Condé,
But what about Easter Monday?
Less mouth-watering is Saint Andrew's Day, noted
for haggis, a dish of which only a Scotsman could
be a condoner,
Since it consists of the heart and liver of a sheep or
calf mixed with oatmeal and suet, boiled in the
stomach of the original owner.
But it's another story on another saint's day, that of

Saint Patrick, not to be confused with Saint Thomas Aquinas,

When we can dig into corned beef and cabbage that instead of parsley is decorated with shamrocks, scientifically known as *Trifolium minus.*

Yes, most feast days provide a fascinating salmagundi,

But again, what about Easter Monday?

Oh, Easter Monday is the day when you long for a magic compound with which your taste buds to inoculate

Because all that's left in the larder is a naked ham bone and a mess of jelly beans and a couple of dozen eggs either hard-boiled and dyed or runny synthetic choculate.

This is a prospect fearsome enough to kill the appetite of a hungry sailor adrift in the Bay of Fundy,

Which is why I call the day after Easter the truly blue, or *sic transit gloria,*
Monday.

THE BIRD LOVER

Keep your cat inside your house,
And I'll stroke his fur and give him a mouse,
But let him loose on my feeding birds
And I'll beat out of him whey and curds.
If into an ornithophile you probe
You'll rouse the sleeping aelurophobe.

BUT I COULD NOT LOVE THEE, ANN, SO MUCH, LOVED I NOT HONORÉ MORE

Some find the world in a grain of sand, I in the correspondence of Ann Landers.

I eavesdrop unabashed as she spoons out her acerb sauce with even hand on lachrymose geese and truculent ganders.

Her desk is positively formicating, which means swarming with moving beings, although I might well employ the other word that sounds like unto it,

Because her mail consists mostly of letters from those embittered ones who have discovered about illicit sex that often there are more headaches than fun to it.

A present-day Emma Lazarus, she cries Give me your huddled problems, the wretched refuse of your wrongs, unwrap for me your festering sores and stigmas;

Your poison is my meat, be it alcoholism, infidelity, frigidity, satyriasis, pre-marital pregnancy or borborygmus.

Yes, if anyone's Gordian love-knot requires a blade more cutting than Alexander's,

Let them call on Ann Landers.

No pussy-footer she, no purveyor of admonitions soothing or polite;

It's Tell the bum to jump in the lake, tell the old bag to go fly a kite.

If Anne of Cleves could have written to Ann Landers

I bet Henry would have thought twice before calling her the mare of Flanders.

From a human comedy as varied as Balzac's I choose for you one excerpt, the ultimate in wails of poignant woe,

The plaint of a teen-ager who doubted the affection of her boy friend because the only compliment he ever paid her was You sweat less than any fat girl I know.

CHILDREN UNDER 12
NO CHARGE,
AND THAT'S TOO MUCH

This year you're going to be as ruthless as Herod and
    as wise as Diogenes,
You're going to take a trip without any papooses or
    offsprings or posterities or progenies.
Neither parental affection nor the benevolent passage
    of time can eclipse
Memories of previous tribal trips,
Such as the interruption to your carefree roaming
The night sweet Alice came down with German
    measles in a hogan outside of Laramie, Wyoming,

And that day next year when Debbie turned alter-
    nately green and yellow,
And threw up continuously from Mount Vernon all
    the way to Monticello.
And the time on the Skyline Drive when little Neddie
    opened the rear door instead of the rear window,
    that morning lingers;
How you frantically pumped the brake while your
    wife clutched him by all there was left of him in
    the car to clutch, his sticky fingers.

Enough said,
Except to mention the visit to Gettysburg and its after-

math, when baby Lucy wept for three days because
Debbie deliberately told her that Lincoln was dead.
Here is where towards your spouse's parents you find
a fresh and compensatory point of view,
It occurs to you that they are not only your father-in-
law and mother-in-law, they are grandparents, too.

If I were given to wagers,
I'd bet a quarter that this year while you are second
honeymooning from motel to luxury motel the little
ones will remain at home being spoiled by those
sentimental pushovers, the Golden Agers.

COEFFICIENTS OF
EXPANSION
(A GUIDE TO THE INFANT SEASON)

What happened in the Hot Stove League last winter?

Well, baseball got a new Commissioner, and the
Senators, who are still the same old Senators al-
though not the original Senators because the orig-
inal Senators are now the Twins, got a new man-
ager, the Splendid Splinter.

Pitchers have been ordered to deliver the ball more
allegro and less adagio,

And if you are wondering about the Royals, well, the
Royals used to be Montreal but now Montreal is
the Expos, and Kansas City, which was the A's,
is the Royals, and the A's, which were first Phila-
delphia and later Kansas City, are Oakland, under
the partial aegis of Joe DiMaggio.

In lower California, confusion is rife around the pot
spots and hot-rodderies;

No one is able to differentiate between San Diego's
twice-born Padres and the Padres' reborn Johnny
Podres.

And, apropos newly launched satellites,

The disappearance of Mickey Mantle was hardly
compensated for by the appearance of something

[21]

called the Pilots, except perhaps to a few Seat-
tleites.*
The mound has been lowered because the hitters
complained that the pitchers were too parsimonious
and pawky,
And Satchel Paige pitched two scoreless exhibition
innings for the Braves of Atlanta, formerly the
Braves of Boston and Milwaukee.
Finally, at least one sportscaster has added a phrase to
his cargo of argot, and I quote him verbatim:
When a batter leaves a runner stranded on third, he
has "failed to plate him."
So, that's how it went.
This wrapup has been brought to you through the
authority of the undersigned Lifelong Fan, and is
not intended in any way to express for the afore-
mentioned expansion said Lifelong Fan's enthu-
siasm, approval, or written consent.

* Since removed to Milwaukee and renamed the Brewers.

THE COLLECTOR

I met a traveler from an antique show,
His pockets empty, but his eyes aglow.
Upon his back, and now his very own,
He bore two vast and trunkless legs of stone.
Amid the torrent of collector's jargon
I gathered he had found himself a bargain,
A permanent conversation piece post-prandial,
Certified genuine early Ozymandial
And when I asked him how he could be sure,
He showed me P. B. Shelley's signature.

A DREAM OF INNOCENT ORGIES
OR, THE MOST UNFORGETTABLE
CHARACTERS I NEVER MET

I'm glad I wasn't ever a Clyde or a Bonnie,
But I'm sorry I was never a stage-door Johnny.
I'd love to have driven down the Gay White Way
In a hansom cab with a big bouquet
To share a bottle and a Chicken Kiev
With a Mitzi Hajos or a Fritzi Scheff
Or a Trixie Friganza —
To squire such dames as,
Glittering names as,
Mitzi Hajos,
Fritzi Scheff,
Or Trixie Friganza.

Had I been born just a little bit earlier,
When ladies of the chorus were voluptuously girlier,
I'm sure I could have fostered in a manner deft
A brotherly acquaintance with the second from the
    left.
But I'd rather have waited for a real bonanza
Like a Fritzi Scheff or a Trixie Friganza
Or a Mitzi Hajos —
To spend my patrimony

Skirting matrimony
With a Fritzi Scheff,
A Mitzi Hajos,
Or a Trixi Friganza.

I'd have overtipped the doormen underneath the
    canopies
Of elegant cafés from Rector's to Bustanoby's.
They'd warn me when a menace appeared upon the
    premises —
Say, a gentleman name of Harry Thaw or lady name
    of Nemesis.
When I heard the chimes at midnight with a Mitzi
    Hajos,
My conduct would have been I hope outrajos . . .
Through all my salad days,
Mardi Gras gala days,
With a Mitzi Hajos,
A Fritzi Scheff,
Or a Trixie Friganza.

Had I only been twenty instead of ten,
I'd have been a legend in Manhattan then,
But temptation was thwarted by the simple truth:
I was just too young to misspend my youth
With a Fritzi Scheff,
A Mitzi Hajos,
A Trixie Friganza,
Or even a Florodora girl.

YES-AND-NO MAN

Poor Manfred, always in bad odor,
Muddled middle-of-the-roader.
Veering Left toward visions bright,
Leftist jargon drives him Right
Until the Rightist hatchet men
Turn him to the Left again,
Searching for a category,
Spo-Radical and desul-Tory.

EARTHLY CREATURES

THE ENTOMORPHICS

Two insects near an Afric bog
Engaged in meaningful dialogue.
Said one, "Tell what the difference are
'Twixt a t-s tsar and a c-z czar."
"The same as are 'twixt you and I,"
Said the tse-tse to the cze-cze fly.

THE COELACANTH

Consider now the Coelacanth,
Our only living fossil,
Persistent as the amaranth,
And status quo apostle.
It jeers at fish unfossilized
As intellectual snobs elite;
Old Coelacanth, so unrevised
It doesn't know it's obsolete.

THE ELK

Moose makes me think of caribou,
And caribou, of moose,
With, even from their point of view,
Legitimate excuse.
Why then, when I behold an elk,
Can I but think of Lawrence Welk?

THE HYENA

Hyena is the kind of beast
I'd not sit down with to a feast.
He is appetite undiscriminating
And mindless laughter unabating.
Slavering in the plush arena,
The studio audience is mostly hyena.

THE LAMPREY

Lampreys are hagfish. In that one word I've said it.
I only know one item to their credit.
The early English had good cause to love them;
Wicked King John died from a surfeit of them.

THE HYLA AND THE BRADYPUS

Said the slothful tree toad to the three-toed sloth,
Is it true you are lazy enough for us both?
I don't bother to scratch even when mosquitoed,
Said the three-toed sloth to the slothful tree toad.

THE CALF

The calf is born with prospects grim,
His life will not be kind to him.
It holds no weal, but only woe,
At home as veal, in France as *veau*.

THE HOG

Some scientist may at last disperse
The mysteries of the universe,

But me, I cannot even think
Why pork is white and ham is pink.

THE SCALLOP

The bivalve mollusk is deemed a treat
Toward which treat-lovers hustle,
Yet it's not the scallop itself they eat,
But the scallop's adductor muscle.
My craving for pot is none of the time,
And for alcohol, sporadic,
But I cannot conceal from the scallop that I'm
An adductor muscle addic.

TO A FOOLISH DOG

Joxer, bouncing harlequin,
All ingratiating grin,
Which begat thee, jolly Joxer?
Airedale, poodle, beagle, boxer?
Scottie braw or Irish terrier?
Never mind, the more the merrier;
A pedigree so heterodox
Perks up thy personality, Jox,
For thou, rambunctious residual,
Wert whelped unique and individual,
A blithe buffoon, a jester pampered,
Nor by the *Ten* Commandments hampered
(I know thou triflest with the Seventh),
But Joxer, mind the stern Eleventh,

Or learn from choking leash and baffling tether
Thy neighbor's Leghorns thou shalt not de-feather.

THE GOSSIP
THAT NEVER SHOULD BE
UNLOOSED IS GOSSIP
THAT CAN'T COME HOME
TO ROOST
(1969)

There are two kinds of gossip, and they differ from
    each other quite a lot,

Because one kind of gossip is sportsmanlike and the
    other kind is definitely not.

This latter kind, shall I tell you what it is?

It is chatter about Ari and Jackie and Mia Farrow and
    the Aga Khan and Vanessa Redgrave and Richard
    and Liz,

About Prince Philip and his domestic financial snarls,

And about the eligibility of mates for the eligible
    Tricia Nixon and the eligible Princess Anne and
    the even eligibler Prince Charles.

It is pregnant with spicy speculation and insinuation
    horrendous,

With innuendo innuendous,

None of which is subject to apology, retraction or
    even discreet voluntary revisal,

Because the gossipers run no risk of retaliation or
    reprisal,

[34]

Because after all, no matter how lurid your hints about Mia or Jackie or Prince Philip or even Tricia,

They don't hear you, so there's no chance they will answer back or sue for slander or call out the militia.

No, the only sportsmanlike gossip is that in which such cozy immunity ends,

It is when you join your best friend in frank confidential discussion of the failings of all your other best friends.

Although you know full well that as long as human nature endures

This best friend will shortly repeat to those best friends your summary of their failings and then join them in a frank confidential discussion of yours.

ROAD BLOCK

Justice has been re-routed
From present to future tense;
The law is so in love with the law
It's forgotten common sense.

THE WARNING

Remember, boy, long as you live,
Gourmet is not an adjective.
Heed my advice, take to your heels,
From the joint that boasts of gourmet meals,
And let its gourmaître dee unleash
His "gourmake-believe" on the nouveaux-riches.

OLDE ENGLANDE, TUSH!
OKAY, U.K.

The Briton he would a-feasting go
On roly-poly, gammon and spinach;
In song and story, but not Soho,
'Twas roly-poly, gammon and spinach.
Now gammon, whatever it is, is spurned
For an entrecôte or a mousse of salmon;
From his clientele mine host has learned
That he cannot serve both Mod and gammon.

FROM AN ANTIQUE LAND

I

When I was ten I didn't want to be president,
Or a woman-wary cowboy like William S. Hart;
I didn't even want to be a fireman.
I wanted to drive a racer a mile a minute.
Where is the sound-effects man to give me the cobble-
  clop of the milkman's horse on Charlton Street,
The lighting expert to capture the glow in the grate,
The wavering kobold dance of shadows on the ceiling?
I sniff again the fringes of smoke from the shifting,
  sifting coals,
Soft and insidious, skunk-like sweet, furring the
  tongue and throat.
Savannah in 1912 hadn't heard of air pollution.
Gulp breakfast now and bundle
Into the bathtub tonneau of the splendid Royal
  Tourist,
It's almost time for the start of the fabulous Grand
  Prize.
The sun has unraveled the mist, but it's cold in the
  wooden stands,
Cold and hard on the bottom.
The mechanics below in the pits pause to blow on
  their fingers.

How vast the machines in the eyes of a little boy!
Strange as gorgons or minotaurs each with its magic
name:
Mercedes, Apperson Jackrabbit, Blitzen Benz, Fiat
and Lozier;
Fiat devil-red, Mercedes and Benz fog-grey,
Apperson blue, and Lozier insipid white,
And for every monster a master, Perseus in helmet
and goggles.
Their names roar by in my mind:
Spenser Wishart, Ralph De Palma,
Bruce Brown and Caleb Bragg
And perhaps another half-dozen of mythopoeic heroes.
Only Barney Oldfield missing;
He never came to Savannah, and we reckoned we
hadn't missed much.
The flag drops, they are off like panicking razorback
hogs,
Under their wheels crushed oyster shell explodes.
Red, blue, grey, and white they streak to the first of
the turns in the highway
Wearily banked for this moment by black men in
black and white stripes.
The driver crowds for position, the spare tire racked
behind him,
At his side his trusty mechanic, pumping oil in a fury.
They vanish around the turn.
How long is the course? Five miles? Ten miles?
It stretches from there to now.

II

When is a Buick not a Buick?

When it's a Skylark? A Le Sabre? A Wildcat, an Electra, a Riviera?

Is it that a Chevrolet is a Chevrolet is a Chevrolet,

Or that a Chevrolet is a Chevy II is a Chevy II Nova is a Chevelle?

You may know a hawk from a handsaw,

But do you know a Plymouth from a Valiant from a Barracuda from a Satellite from a Fury from a Road Runner?

Fooled again; it's all of them.

You've decided to buy a Ford, or perhaps an Oldsmobile, a Mercury, Dodge, a Pontiac, a Rambler;

Pick your Rambler, your Pontiac, your Dodge, your Mercury, Oldsmobile, Ford from among the following:

Mustang, Comet, Montego, Firebird, Cougar, Bronco, Charger, Galaxie, Rebel, Tempest, Falcon, Rogue, Polara and Toronado.

Go ahead, pick the one you want, assuming you can identify it;

Then tell me who made it.

I remember the one-name cars, the cars you could tell apart.

I remember the Panhard, with a sort of lid on legs on top of the hood;

Pierce Arrow, its headlights spraddled on the mud-
guards.
They didn't look like the Mercer, nor the Mercer the
Marmon,
The Hupp like the Franklin nor the Franklin like the
Reo.
You knew the Pope-Hartford from the Pope-Toledo,
The Simplex from the Stanley, and all from the black
Tin Lizzie.
Some were steamers, some air-cooled and some chain-
driven,
But each as individual as a fingerprint.
You strained the gas through a chamois rag,
And half the grown-ups had broken wrists from the
kick of the crank,
And the roadsters looked fine with a collie on the run-
ning board.
I see where a fellow paid $45,000 for a 1913 Mercer
Runabout.
I wonder how old he was . . .

GIVE-AWAY, GIVE-AWAY, BANKER MAN

We have an agreement with the bank.
They don't sell drinks, we don't cash checks.
— Sign in old-time saloon

O Merchants, why do your profits wane?
The Banker is raiding your domain.
His advertisements are grim foreboders
Of the race to attract alert free-loaders.
Take your dollars, he hollers, and head point-blank
For the nearest philanthropic bank.
Just mosey in through the big front door
And walk out in a jiffy with either/or *A Color TV, a*
   Movie Camera, a Lighted Cosmetic Mirror and
   Electric Manicure Set, a Double Hibachi, a Mar-
   ble Cheese Tray or an 18-piece Cotton Layette Set.
O ye of Macy and ye of Gimbel,
Refrain from famous rivalry nimble,
And if to stay in business ye hanker
Make a pact with your friendly banker.
Swear upon your auditor's bones
You won't handle mortgages, won't make loans,
If he, when once the pact is made,
Will stop giving away your stock-in-trade.

GOOSE POPULATION
GAINS HIGH LEVEL

Headline (New York Times)

Besides pollution and erosion
We now must face a goose explosion.
A glut of geese can play the devil
With national life on every level,
Especially in politics,
Where geese and government intermix.
This solemn thought I introduce:
The higher the level, the bigger the goose.

GUESS WHAT I'D RATHER BE THAN A TENDER APPLE BLOSSOM

When comforts flee, as the hymnist wrote, and other
helpers fail,
I meditate on the whale.
The whale is a creature many selfish people have an
idée fixe on,
They see it only as a source of whalebone for their
canaries to sharpen their beaks on.
Such people are either out of touch with the world
of whales or deficient in Intelligence Quotient;
They are unaware of a fact that a scientific
underwater investigator has recently uneartht, or
should I say, unoceant.
If these ignoramuses ever have a thought, here is
food for it:
Whales can sing the same as canaries, and they don't
need to rub their noses on canary bone to be put in
the mood for it:
What are the songs that whispereth, whimpereth or
whistleth the whale when singing?
I like to think, Perhaps the same the sirens sang to
drive mast-bound Odysseus mad with longing.
Modern whales congregate in gams or pods, as in the
days when Moby-Dick the ocean swam,

And the *Pequod's* lookout cried on sighting them, as
Melville prudishly refrained from recording, not
"Hot dog!" but "Pod gam!"
I take issue with a certain hard-shell fundamentalist in
South Dakota, town of Yankton;
He says whales eat people, but they don't, they eat
plankton.
Whales, like us, were once fish, and they came ashore
just long enough to become mammals;
Indeed, the hump-backed whales, genus *Megaptera*,
got back in the water barely in time to avoid becom-
ing camels.
Yes, whales took one look at what was going on on
land and plumped for the sea, any sea, from the
Arctic to the Caribbean,
As God knows so would I, were I only amphibian.

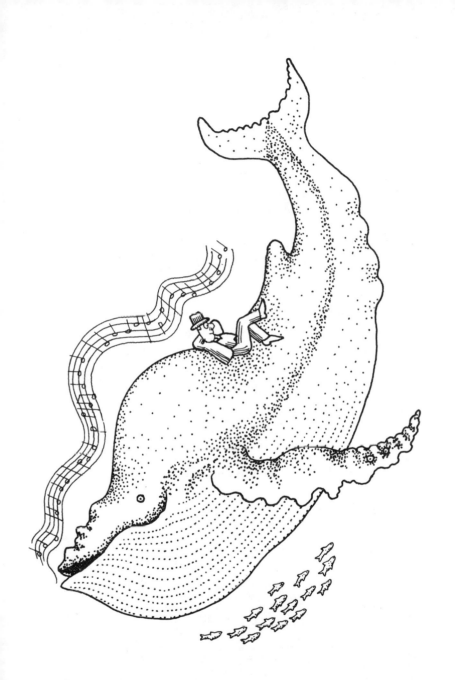

H'AVE, CAESAR,
OR, BOADICEA'S REVENGE

The Italian language is so musical as to be a veritable
  concerto,
In which to me the only discord is that Italians play
  fast and loose with their h's and call people Ugo
  instead of Hugo and decapitate Humbert into
  Umberto.
Yes, and their Roman ancestors, although noted for
  their precise and orderly natures,
They too were capricious and undependable h'ers.
In a moment of idle speculation I asked myself why
  sometimes Hadrian was Adrian and Heliogabalus
  Elagabalus,
And I came up with an answer that rang the bell with
  a clangor resonant and tintinnabalous.
It occurred to me that there might have been a num-
  ber of centurions who had been stationed too long
  in Londinium,
And when they got back to Rome they were saying
  "larkspur" instead of "delphinium."
This was sad enough, but what it indicated was sadder
  even than the tale of Philomela and Procne;
They had gone Cockney.
This was evident in their use of nomenclature;

They spoke of the h'Odes of 'Orace, thus deviating
from customary Romenclature.
They called for a pint of 'arf-and-'arf rather than a
goblet of Falernian to get a glow on,
And in brushing up on their declensions they said
"'ic, 'aec, 'oc, 'uius, 'uius, 'uius" and so on.
I believe it is these h'Antonius Weller type Romans
whose tongue the modern Italian is heir to,
And that is why Hugo turns up as Ugo and Hum-
bert is decapitated into Umberto.

HE DIDN'T DARE LOOK,
OR, THE PUZZLING UNIQUENESS
OF MR. SALTBODY'S MEEKNESS

I speak of Standish Saltbody, Harvard '24, a loyal
    Cantabridgin,
A timid man, a bashful man, whose makeup con-
    tained of arrogance not a modicum or a smidgin.
You would travel far to discover a character more
    retiring, more innately diffident,
His overdeveloped sense of self-unimportance was
    pathetically evident,
Yet in him a kindred soul is what Galileo's persecutors
    might well have found
Because his very timidity led him to fear that Standish
    Saltbody was what the universe revolved around.
Small wonder that he was continually discomfited
    by a runaway pulse;
He was convinced that his most trivial act could gen-
    erate the most appalling results.
He had not once attended the Yale game since under-
    going graduation and valedictory
Because he was sure that his presence alone, although
    unsuspected by his team, was sufficient to guarantee
    an Eli victory.
Although Willie Mays was his hero, his very ideal, he
    would never watch him on TV

Because he was sure that although Willie couldn't
    know that Standish Saltbody was watching him
    from a distance of 2500 miles, that one fact would
    hoodoo him into looking at strike three.
His sense of responsibility and guilt reached a point at
    which from any positive move he was likely to re-
    frain;
He was certain that any candidate he voted for would
    be defeated, just as his washing the car would bring
    on a torrential rain.
Thus we see that this meekest and most self-deprecia-
    tive of God's creatures paradoxically felt himself to
    be omnipotent,
Since of any contretemps in his immediate world his
    words or deeds were obviously the precipitant;
And indeed, if of the cosmos he was not the hub,
How is it that he could make the telephone ring
    merely by settling down in the tub?

HIGH, LOW THE COMEDY:
A WINTER'S TALE

Ice from the leaking hill glints on the terrace below.
My sunflower seed speckles the crusty snow.
High-perched on the white-topped wall, cardinal
    aflame,
Like one of Braddock's redcoats, easy game,
Come-kill-me target for all his absurd disguise,
Sun-fielder's sooty smudge around defensive eyes.
Vulnerable is cautious; timid, severe;
He orders mate to alight, prove the coast clear.
Hungry he watches, first pecks no lurking peril reveal.
Down he flutters, drives her off, approaches his meal.
Behind frozen azalea cat crouches, twitches,
Pupil and teacher of a hundred witches,
Here's insolence and ancient arrogance; he's sleek
With confidence, fierce whiskers boasting from each
    cheek.
Low-bellied he tenses muscles, springs in beauty hate-
    ful.
Balefire he fears not, knows not ice to footing fateful.
Cardinal flies away, saved by skidding cat-fall.
I shudder, as watching Lucifer do a pratfall.

IF ETHYL VANILLIN
BE THE FOOD OF LOVE,
DRINK ON

What reduces a maiden fair
To a rag and a bone and a hank of hair?
Not overwork, as you might surmise,
Or a broken heart, or exercise,
But a magic potion by chemists brewed
On which they exist instead of food.
The tipple to which they pledge allegiance
Contains the following ingregiance:

> Dibasic calcium phosphate
> And ferric orthophosphate,
> As well as manganese sulphate
> And ammonium carrageenan,
> A pinch of sodium caseinate
> And sodium ascorbate
> Plus the sodium superb,
> Known as silico-aluminate.

O maidens fair, as long as you want
To be cylindrical and gaunt
I won't suggest such natural nutriments
As steak and its fattening accoutrements,
I'll not oppose with tongue or pen
Your cadaverous chemical regimen,

[55]

Your emaciation is what I quaff to,
But not, dear maidens, unless I haff to

In a mug of riboflavin
With of lecithin a soupçon,
With calcium pantothenate
And thiamine mononitrate,
A dash of potassium iodide
And cyanocobalamin,
And lastly, for bouquet,
Pyrodoxine hydrochloride.

Fair maidens swigging in a row,
They are chemicals from tip to toe.
Young men, you risk a fit, a conniption,
If you kiss one without a doctor's prescription.

IS THIS ANY WAY
TO ADVERTISE AN AIRLINE?
YOU BET IT IS!

Consider the thoughts of Darius Green
When he'd finished inventing his flying machine
A problem arose at which he boggled,
He said to himself, I'll be hornswoggled!
Yup, I'll be a son of a shogun;
What's an airline without a slogan?
How kin a feller attract a mob
Aboard this newfangled thingumabob?
Can't say it will start on time jest so,
Or land you at where you aimed to go;
You couldn't call it comf'table, strickly,
Can't say it's safe, fer it ain't, pertickly;
Don't keer to skeer the folks away;
What in tarnation *kin* I say?
The only solution, looks to me,
Is a slogan harmless as sassafras tea.
Up, up and away is a tasty vittle,
It's optimistic but non-committal,
Or, *Come on down!* That's fair and square,
They sartinly will, sometime, somewhere;
Or, *Darius Makes the Goin' Great* —
Speshly after a two-hour wait —
Since the Lord ain't hostile to the pious,

Fly friendly skies with devout Darius.
But afore the campaign will truly gee,
Reckon I'll have to invent TV
And borrer that vaudeville joke, gal ding it!
Ef suthin's too silly to say, you sing it.

IS THERE A DR. JOHNSON
IN THE HOUSE?

Do you know with whom I feel a temperamental kin-
    ship? I will tell you with whom —
It is Dr. Johnson who said, "Tomorrow I purpose to
    regulate my room."
That statement has a valiant sound to it,
But, being a temperamental kinsman of his, I bet he
    never got around to it.
Myself in a similar situation I daily find;
Tomorrow I purpose to regulate my mind.
My mind to me a refuse heap is, of odds and bodkins,
    of snips and snails, of scraps and shards;
It is as useful to me as a deck of fifty-one cards.
I often tend to forget my home telephone number and
    even my own surname, or patronymic,
Probably because I am so busy remembering that Ben-
    jamin Harrison was married first to Caroline La-
    vinia Scott and later to Mrs. Mary Scott Dimmick.
When I try to recall a tune that I like, my memory is
    dormant in Ephesus with the Seven Sleepers,
The only tunes I can remember are ones I detest, such
    as "Love Is a Many-Splendored Thing" and "Jeep-
    ers Creepers, Where'd Ya Get Those Peepers?"
I can give you the date (1689) of the Toleration Act
    in favor of the Dissenters, as well as the Act of

Grace, because I am so knowledgeable, speaking
William and Mary–wise,
But I drive blocks out of my way because I forget
whether Manhattan's even-numbered streets are
westbound and the odd-numbered eastbound, or
contrariwise.
Coming up with useful information is a feat that my
mind is less than quick at,
But as for things I'd just as soon never have known,
it is so full of them that it is like the orchestra that
had more musicians in it than the conductor could
shake a stick at.

THE MADCAP ZOOLOGIST

Adam was a simple man,
Inept at parlor games,
So when he named the animals,
He gave them simple names,
Like mouse and moose
And duck and goose
And dog and goat
And horse and shoat,
And sheep and cow and lamb and calf,
And lion, tiger and giraffe;
For each he chose a simple label
To teach to little Cain and Abel.
Yes, Adam did his simple best,
And then to Eve he left the rest.
So along came Eve,
And you'd never believe
The names that she had up her sleeve.
No easily memorized names for her,
No cats or rats or bats, no sir!
Her mind, though recently created,
Was femininely complicated.
At a time when the Dog Star was just a pup,
Here are some of the names she conjured up:
At first, in a jiffy, a trice, a whisk,
She invented the guib and the bassarisk,

And, in the twinkling of an eye,
The chickaree and the chigetai.
Then, ever stranger, ever abstruser,
Coypu, poyou and babirusa,
And ever abstruser, ever stranger,
Grivet, angwantibo, phalanger.
Oh, many a quaint idea she had,
Such as dingo, dugong and aoudad.
As result of a kind of mental judo,
Came foumart, pangolin and peludo.
In her nomenclatural panorama
Were urial, zoril and mazama,
Plus mysterious creatures called tatou pebas,
The thought of which gives me the heeba-jeebas.
The moral is this: Remember, boys,
As long as the old earth whirls,
When the quarrel proceeds to calling names,
You'll never catch up to the girls.

I WONDER WHAT THEY
BROUGHT FROM GHENT
TO AIX

My newspaper in winter helps light the fire but it
doesn't help warm the depths of my heart, collo-
quially known as cockles.

The front page is a showcase of dire disasters, doom-
ful doings and dismal debacles.

The entertainment section is of my dejected mood no
alleviator or temperer;

Such are the current movies that even the printed
pitch for them would add a blush to the painted
cheek of a degenerate Roman emperor.

On the society page the Croesus-cum-Arts group has
taken over *noblesse oblige* with no ifs or buts;

The popping of corks mingles with the cries of Burn,
baby, burn! till you can't tell the chic from the guts.

The sports page is as thrilling as a lecture on bimet-
allism by Winnie-the-Pooh;

Nothing there but basketball, a game which won't be
fit for people until they set the basket umbilicus-
high and return the giraffes to the zoo.

The columnists five times a week on what the admin-
istration might do or should do pontificate and
speculate,

And each believes that of the truth his own conception is alone immaculate.

And don't forget that blight on the ballot, the poll weevil.

I often wish that the film could be reversed and my newspaper could turn back first to pulp and then to murmuring pines and hemlocks and I could carve Everybody go home on their trunks in the forest primeval.

MEN'S LIB
AD LIB

Maxi midi mini,
Hear the ladies whinny!
Mini maxi midi,
Gentlemen grow giddy.
Mini midi maxi!
I'm off to Cotopaxi —
TAXI!

MINI-JABBERWOCKY

Most people would find rising unemployment
A source of unenjoyment.
Not so the anonymous presidential advisor
Whose comment might have been wiser.
He has informed the nation
That rising unemployment is merely a statistical
    aberration.
I don't want to argue or squabble,
But that gook I won't gobble.

THE MOPING MINSTREL

O, the secret sorrow of Calvin Coy,
America's favorite minstrel boy!
His ratings top the topmost ten,
His records are hotter than hot cayenne.
In accord with TV protocol
He has a house like the Taj Mahal,
A regal Rolls and a modest Bentley
And a Cord that he treasures sentimently,
   And Bing has been his guest star,
   And Bob has been his guest star,
   And Glen has been his guest star,
   And Andy has been his guest star,
And he, in established modus operandi,
Has guested for Bing and Bob and Glen and Andy.
What then is the sorrow of Calvin Coy,
That disarmingly boyish minstrel boy?
What is the source of the tear that clings
To the bridge of the nose through which he sings?
Though he has his Abolish Anthrax telethon,
There is one sore point that his ego dwelleth on.
He won't feel secure upon his throne
Till he has a tournament all his own.
   For Bing's got a tournament,
   And Bob's got a tournament,

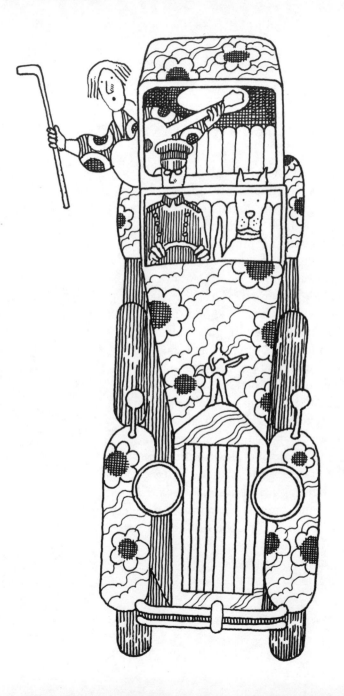

And Glen's got a tournament,
And Andy's got a tournament,
While Calvin Coy, the winsome, wholesome, glee-
some,
Can't get to sponsor so much as a pick-up threesome.

Yet St. Andrew's might gie him a Royal and Ancient
tartan
Should he wangle to sponsor a tourney omitting Dean
Martin.

MOST DOCTORS RECOMMEND,
OR, YOURS FOR FAST FAST FAST RELIEF

They say that when cigarette advertising was banned
    from the air the networks lost a cool billion in
    billing,

And at first they felt like their tooth had just lost a
    filling,

But they soon reflected that the cavity would be more
    than refilled with a rich amalgam of et cetera such
    as laxatives and deodorants,

And they viewed the situation with more forebear-
    ance and less foreboderance.

They said it might have been worse, and drank to the
    future in Smirnoff or Beefeater or Gilbey.

They said it might have been worse; I say that with
    any luck it will be.

When it comes to supposing, I am a man without a
    scruple,

So let us suppose that in the first year off the air the
    consumption of cigarettes should double or quad-
    ruple.

Would not the producers of other goods begin to think
    twice?

And wouldn't that be nice?

Good wine needs no bush,

And perhaps products that people really want need no
    hard-sell or soft-sell TV push.

Why not?
Look at pot.

THE MUSEUM OF
NATURAL HISTORY

Now let us all, from egghead to barbarian,
Salute our newest, noblest centenarian.
Yea, let proud princely prelates in consistory
Exalt the living spirit of Natural History,
And raise their voices in a vast Te Deum
And Alleluias for our own Museum.
No Johnny-come-lately, this, or upstart parvenu,
Crammed down Consumers' throats by Madison
    Avenue,
But all the ages in one ageless shrine
Built by man's curiosity divine.
How infinite is life, and how protean,
In halls where time is measured by the aeon,
And man beholds in form that ever varies
His predecessors and contemporaries.
I'd like to show you a little of what's inside
If you'll have an ignoramus as your guide.

TYRANNOSAURUS REX

Tiny tots of either sex
Adore Tyrannosaurus Rex.
Indeed, all little ones adore
Any savage carnivore,

[74]

Of which, O Rex, thou rightly boastest,
Thou art not only first, but mostest.

THE WHALE

Behold the sulphur-bottom whale,
Some 25 yards from nose to tail.
I find it somewhat ludicrous
That whales are mammals, just like us,
And basking where the plankton teems
They dream their sweet cetacean dreams.
One dreaming sulphur-bottom chick
In her Maidenform bra met Moby-Dick.

THE PYTHON

The python has, and I fib no fibs,
318 pairs of ribs.
In stating this I place reliance
On a seance with one who died for science.
This figure is sworn to and attested;
He counted them while being digested.

ROCK ROOM

Outside the hall of quartz and crystal
You're asked to kindly check your pistol,
For Star of India here is seen,
That gem of purist ray serene,
So Orientally entrancing
That it would set a ranee dancing,

And when it comes within his view
The guru leaps like a kan-guru.

THE HALL OF PRIMATES

Here condescending viewers feel behooved
To acknowledge their cousins many times removed.
It's a family reunion of us primates
Transported here from countless realms and climates.
All other mammals they're distinguished from
By grasping fingers and apposable thumb.
Primates evolve in many curious shapes,
Monkeys and aye-ayes, lemurs, pottos, apes,
But for perfection one alone earns credit;
Man is the premier primate. He has said it.

NOBODY'S PERFECT,
ARE THEY,
BUT WOULDN'T IT BE NICE?

One is definitely paunchy.
One's figure would draw sneers from Bill Blass or
  Givenchy.
One reads of magic belts
Beneath which the waistline melts.
No comment-arousers,
They are worn under the trousers.
No diet grim, no calisthenics grimmer;
One simply dons the belt and grows inches slimmer.
One envisions oneself as cigarette-thin, a veritable
  faun.
One orders the belt and puts it on.
One's middle is indeed magically compressed.
Then one starts to get dressed.
End of romance.
The belt has more than replaced the bulk it elim-
  inated, and over it one cannot button one's pants.
That's the dilemma facing obese daydreamers and
  drowsers;
Which shall it be, the trousers without the belt or the
  belt without the trousers?

The belt is as advertised, and in shorts the wearer
　　looks athletically trim in one;
What one now needs is to reduce enough so that one
　　can get one's pants on over it so that it can begin
　　to slimmen one.

NO TROUBLE AT ALL,
IT'S AS EASY AS FALLING OFF
A PORTABLE BAR

I often appeal to the Lord of hosts, because a host I
often find myself,
And to the frustrations of hostmanship I cannot blind
myself.
I invariably fail the ultimate test:
Outguessing the guest.
Would that I could anticipate
How my guests will elect to dissipate.
Now ice and glasses glisten within easy reach,
The guests old friends, the liquors lined up on the bar
in accordance with the well-known taste of each.
Comes Polyhymnia, the semi-teetotaller for whom you
have bought her favorite brand of sherry;
Tonight she would like just straight bourbon on the
rocks with perhaps a little sugar and bitters and, if
it's not too much trouble, a slice of orange and a
maraschino cherry.
And Alistair, his cheek by years of aged Scotch all
motley mottled —
Beefeater gin for him with just an ounce and a half
of lime juice, preferably British-bottled.
Here's Otho, a Martini man as sure as da Gama's
name was Vasco;

He'll take a Bloody Mary, only with a tequila base and
maybe an extra dash of Worcestershire sauce and
lemon and just two drops of Tabasco.
And Ethel, for whose sole benefit a stock of Dubonnet
you carry —
This time she requests Campari.
Wilfred is smugly off the stuff, so you have provided
every current alternative or proxy;
He declines tomato juice, ginger ale, Coke, Sprite,
Squirt, Fresca, and Bitter Lemon, and wistfully
supposes you haven't anything in the way of Bevo
or Moxie.
At long last Lily, surely fairest flower of the lot;
You ask her what she would like, and she replies,
"Oh, anything at all, dear, what have you got?"
Well, I'll tell you what I've got and what she's going
to get this time, by cracky:
My customary apéritif, pawpaw juice and *sake*.

ONE MAN'S OPIATE

In the *Affendämmerung,* or twilight of the apes,
What is more fitting than that man should for reas-
surance turn to japes?
In chaos sublunary
What remains constant but buffoonery?
I know of a man named Daniel Deronda
And of buffoonery he is a veritable Golconda.
Once he was sipping a *fine* in a café in Montmartre,
When a man sat down at his table who wanted to
discuss Sartre.
Daniel didn't wish to discuss Sartre, whose works
filled him with ennui;
He told himself, "Dan, we can't put up with ennui,
can we?"
So he said, *"Frappe, frappe,"* and the man said, *"Qui
va là?"* and he said, *"Alençon,"* and the man said,
"Alençon qui?"
And Daniel said, *"Alençonfants de la patrie."*
The Sartre man, himself a lacemaker, was so taken
aback that instead of exclaiming, *"Ma fwah!"* ("My
faith!"), *il s'écria,* "Mon *fwah!"* which every goose
knows means "My liver!"
And then threw himself into the Seine, a river.
I'm all for Daniel: In this age penumbral,
Let the timbrel resound in the tumbrel.

PIX SHEETS TOP
KEATS FEATS

I yearn, should Fate the favor give,
To find one brave new adjective,
An adjective as fresh and apt
As apple pie with ice cream capped.
Yet if I found one, snickers Fate,
I would have come on it too late,
For none's forgotten quite so soon
As him who's fourth to walk the moon.
Frustration-fraught am I, am galled,
Since in my quest I've been forestalled.

John Wasserman, trenchant and laconical,
Critic for San Francisco *Chronicle*,
Reviewing *Censorship in Denmark*,
Gains immortality with one penmark,
Writes without fussy pedagoggling,
"Mind-boggling!"

In *Cosmopolitan*, Liz Smith,
Phrase-maker to be reckoned with.
She looks at *Rider in the Rain*,
Coins gold that glows in Memory Lane,
Adjective-wise and feminine-angling:
"Jaw-dangling!"

In reverence turn to *City East*
Where Newton North as pundit priest
Describes the caper *Kelly's Heroes*
In terms that pack the punch of Spiro's,
Words walloping, rocking, socking, jabbing:
"Gut-grabbing!"

I'm faint with jealousy and awe,
With boggled mind and dangled jaw,
And, spreading from entrail unto entrail,
An ecstasy of agony ventral.
I fizzle like an ebbing siphon;
Couldn't even invent the hyphen.

PLEASE REMIND ME
BEFORE I FORGET

MEMORY CONTROL BELIEVED LOCATED

> The ridge of the human brain
> called the hippocampus seems to
> preside over the memory. . . . Ex-
> periments have shown that when
> the hippocampus is interfered
> with, recent memory and ability
> to learn new things is impaired.
> — *The Times.*

I had laid my growing forgetfulness to anno Domini,
To which I was prepared to surrender in ignominy;
I was grovelling in acquiescence to senescence.
This delayed bulletin from the *Times* is a tonic
For humiliation over my failings mnemonic.
I now know that memory has not completely fled —
It's just that I have this hippocampus in my head,
And to maintain such a lodger is nothing mere,
Nothing trivial like a bee in the bonnet or a flea in
    the ear.
Because what is a hippocampus?
According to Webster, it's a fabulous monster with
    head and forequarters like a horse and a tail like a
    dolphin or possibly a grampus.
Small wonder I forget which was the bad guy, the
    Virginian or Trampas —

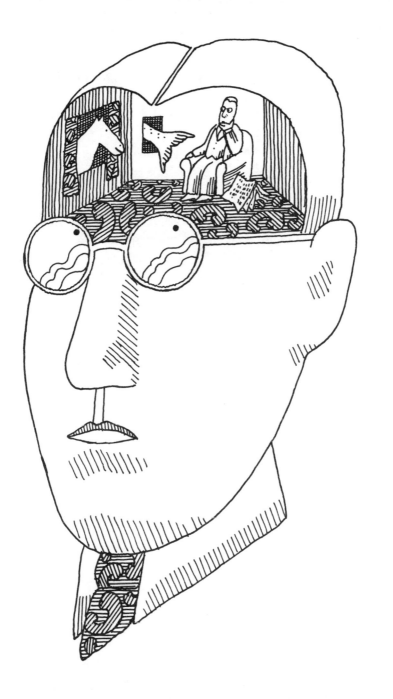

Someone's been messing around with my hippo-
campus.

Do I confuse the Black Bull of Norroway with the
Wild Bull of the Pampas?

Run the saliva test on my hippocampus.

Do I disremember which are the finer cigars, Havanas
or Tampas?

Disqualify my hippocampus.

The *Times* further states that an intimate role in the
memory process is that of neuroglia, the supporting
tissue of the brain,

From any comment on which I shall refrain.

The hippocampus is enough to carry in my mind;
should I add a hippocampus-neuroglia-imbroglio,

My mind would boggleyo.

What is it that if added to my hippocampus I should
regret it?

Gracious, my hippocampus has already caused me to
forget it!

POLITICAL REFLECTION

Discretion is the better part of virtue;
Commitments the voters don't know about can't hurt
you.

RECITATIFS NEVER TO BE RECITED AT LINCOLN CENTER FOR THE PERFORMING ARTS

STAGE

Whatever you may think of the latest Hamlet, one
thing is certain,
He owes nothing to Barrymore or Evans or Burton,
None of whom appeared
Accoutred with bracelet and beads and beard,
And all of whom from grooviness were truants,
Never realizing that between yeah yeah yeah and yeh
yeh yeh there is a subtle nuance.
This Hamlet not only *plays* Hamlet he *is* Hamlet,
convincing in his tragic oddness;
I can but conclude that there is Method in his Mod-
ness.

DANCE

Once there was a famous *première danseuse* and also
   an equally famous whatever you call her male
   equivalent,

And their feelings toward one another were far from
   benevolent.

Their mutual insults came not as single spies but in
   platoons;

She said that his musical preference was occasionally
   Bach but more Offenbach, and he said that she
   thought Massenet occurred on Wednesday and
   Saturday afternoons.

But it was their *pas de deux* that could whip up a
   tempest in a samovar in an inkling,

They bickered incessantly over whose toes were the
   more twinkling.

After each *pas de deux* the battle raged to and fro
   and pro and con;

Once she, having learned her American in England,
   expressed her opinion of his performance with a
   disgusted Well I swan, and he said, You mean
   lousily you swan,

And she said, You wouldn't dare say that if my father
   were here,

And he said, My *pas* can lick your *pas* any day, and
   Diaghilev overheard this interchange and it ended
   both their career.

SYMPHONY

We parents are forever complaining that our children
    will not obey us.

I think immediately of the outstandingly recalcitrant
    child of Herr and Frau Mozart, young Wolfgang
    Amadeus.

People often ask me why, if the infant Mozart was
    such a prodigy, he didn't compose "O Tannen-
    baum" and "Stille Nacht."

Well, let me tell you about the birthday which found
    him six years old and never been Spocked.

His parents, as generous as they were kind and true,

Presented him with not one harpsichord but two,

A harpsichord grand from his father and an upright
    from his mother,

And they suggested that he compose "Stille Nacht"

on one and "O Tannenbaum" on the other,

And he flew into a tantrum, he should have been
    plunged into a cold bath with all his clothes on,

And he screamed that he wouldn't compose anything
    on those *Gottverdammte* instruments, he wanted
    good old harpsichords to compose on,

And they assured him that it *was* harpsichords they
    had given him, they employed the strongest terms
    they dared to,

And he said, I say it's spinets and I say the hell with
    it, and he left "Stille Nacht" and "O Tannenbaum"
    to be composed by anyone who cared to.

REFLECTION ON
BAREFOOT HOSTESS
WITH CHEEK OF TAN

Man wants but little here below,
And least of all the female toe.

REFLECTION ON THE
DECORATION DETESTABLE

I execrate in the drink I quaff
A maraschino, whole or half,
And heaven knows the pains I take
To scrape it off ice cream or cake.
This cloying artificial sweet
Is sickly to look at, worse to eat.
Thus, when at table I orate
The maraskeynote is one of hate.

REFLECTION ON
HOSPITAL HOSPITALITY

One eats no meats,
Just Jell-O and beets,
And soups,
And schloops of Cream of Wheats.

THE REJECTED PORTRAIT

Mr. Danvers in the chair
Runs his fingers through his hair,
Gives his chest a manly heave
And smoothes the wrinkles in his sleeve.
The empty backside of the canvas
A mirror is to Mr. Danvers
In which he may with cunning ferrety
Rehearse his meeting with posterity.
He must his part as brilliant play
As a Gielgud or Olivier.
Just what should the expression be
To catch the essential Mr. D.?
Emotions stumble across his face
Like kids in a potato race.
See how his facial muscles work
Lest whimsical smile become a smirk.
Now he is frowning, now he's quizzical,
Now meditative or metaphysical.
Watch him in fleeting roles consecutive,
Athlete, musician, stern executive.
Oddly, of all his parts the oddest
Is that in which he's playing modest.
The painter, who's been there before,
He knows what mummeries to ignore;

Somehow, from under each mad grimace
He excavates a human face.
Then where's the genuine Mr. Danvers?
Not in the chair, but on the canvas.

THE REWARD

In my mind's reception room
Which is what, and who is whom?
I notice when the candle's lighted
Half the guests are uninvited,
And oddest fancies, merriest jests,
Come from these unbidden guests.

THE SAD CASE OF THE
EXPATRIATE SOCIALITE,
OR, IT'S NEVER IN THE PHRASE BOOK

Once there was a Manhattan socialite named Stella
    Maris,
And her French was formidable in Manhattan but not
    in Paris.
Manhattan headwaiters responded to her French with
    suavity to spare.
Not so in *La Ville Lumière*.
At her socially impeccable school she had passed her
    college boards and had read Corneille and Molière,
But in Paris even her request for a glass of water was
    answered by a humiliating stare.
Should she offer a taxi driver a cigarette with a halt-
    ing Voulez-vous fumer he understands her at once,
    but should she then ask to be taken to the Boule-
    vard Haussmann or even the Champs Elysées,
Why he is as stonily uncomprehending as a rock fan
    listening to *Les Pêcheurs de Perles* by Alexandre
    César Léopold Bizet.
She grows more and more like Burns's mouse, timid,
    cowerin' and sleekit;
Her schooling has taught her everything about French
    except how to speak it.
What boots her now her term paper on Racine?

When in need of a stimulant she can't remember
whether to ask for *un fine* or *une fine*.
You'll be glad to know that she has now recognized
the problem of gender and in a state of mild but
permanent inebriety has learned to dwell with it;
These days she orders *deux fines,* and the hell with it.
There is a precedent for her action set by Madame de
Rambouillet,
Who, I have been told, always demanded a double
Drambuie.

A GOOSE FOR THE SAUCE

Oh how greedy Mr. Cross is!
He's simply mad about rich sauces.
From overindulgence in a bordelaise
He's apt to end up drunk and disordelaise,
But the sauce he awards a big A plus
Is made by a friend who drives a bus.
On vacation during the ragweed and pollen days
He enjoys a busman's hollandaise.

SEXUAL POLITICS FAREWELL:
A MEMO TO KATE MILLETT,
SHULAMITH FIRESTONE, BETTY FRIEDAN
ET AL. (AL. STANDS FOR ALICE,
NOT ALBERT)

Ladies, the war is over, the battle of the sexes is terminated, yours is the victorious gender.
Herewith please find my unconditional surrender.
Although I lay down my arms, although I am now only a missile without a warhead,
I am neither a crybaby nor a sorehead.
I realize that for centuries, for ages, yes, for eons,
You were our vassals, our slaves, our peons.
We grew complacent, we grew lazy and slumberous;
Little did we reck that you were preparing to outnumber us.
It was a bloodless war, not a crude war,
But imperceptibly you infiltrated such masculine strongholds as the ballot and the bank account, the highball and the highway, the lobby and the lab, the college and the country club, while emerging from the kitchen and the boudoir.
Not only are more of you born but most of you outlive us;
As Isaiah prophesied, the day has come when seven

women shall take hold of one man, and I can only
hope that for our past tyranny you will forgive us.
We are the vanquished, we dare not argue, you can
forever say good riddance
To those perpetual spousely spats full of "Yes I dids"
and "No you didn'ts."
Farewell, a long farewell to marital fuss;
To the victor belong the spoils, which is us.
Ladies triumphant, at your feet our fate we fearfully
lay;
Although we are guilty we trust that you will be
lenient and not continue to prosecute us like a
headline-hunting District Attorney, or what I call
a Ta-ra-ra boom D.A.

THE SLIPSHOD SCHOLAR
GETS AROUND TO GREECE

I sing of the ancient Greeks.
They had magnificent physiques.
They were also intellectual Titans,
And wore chlamyses and chitons.
Their minds were serene unless too much success
    induced hubris,
In which case the gods rendered them lugubrous.
They were preeminent in art and science,
And in their pottery they anticipated faïence.
Indeed they were our precursors in many ways; just
    think how their man Homer did Milton and
    Tennyson precurse:
Because he could not think of a rhyme for orange he
    invented blank verse.
Even the Stock Exchange reflects their far-off light;
Had the Greeks not bequeathed us their language,
    brokers would be trading not in AT&T but in
    American Distantsound & Distantwrite.
If the Greeks had never existed who would have
    been the most annoyed?
Freud.
Without their drama where would he have uncovered
    all those complexes,

His pop-plexes and mom-plexes?

The path of Oedipus into the annals of analysis was straight, Electra's rather more tortuous.

I shall try to map it for you though I may evoke offended cries of *De mortuis*.

Electra persuaded her brother, Orestes, to murder their mother, Clytemnestra, who had persuaded her lover, Aegisthus, to murder Agamemnon, their father, whom Electra loved like billy-o,

And Orestes did in fact murder Clytemnestra and her lover with classic punctilio.

Thus was Agamemnon avenged and his adulterous slayers eradicated.

The Greek words for Electra were Accessory Before the Fact, but Dr. Freud and I think of her simply as a daughter who was over-daddycated.

SPEAK TO ME ONLY WITH THINE EYES, AND PLEASE, NOT TOO FAST

There are countries where being multilingual is of no
  advantage to the tourist,
Because no matter how impeccable his grammar and
  idiom the natives refuse to understand him unless
  his accent and inflection are of the purist.
Of course there is another side to the coin;
Maltreatment of a foreign tongue does not always
  lead to a *coup de pied* in the groin —
Consider the case of one Mr. Ruthuen, an avid col-
  lector of art.
Once he was motoring through Germany and with
  every mile he took his Americanism more deeply to
  heart.
He felt that to speak German as do the Germans
  would be to bootlick,
So although he could perfectly well have said *gemüt-
  lich* he always said gemootlick.
One day he got lost on a primitive country road,
And he stopped to query a typical old charcoal burner
  who was smoking a meerschaum pipe outside his
  humble abode,

And he asked for the Autobahn in his customary per-
emptory tone,
And five minutes later he resumed his journey carry-
ing with him a superb Audubon, hitherto un-
known.

SWEET LAND OF CAPITALS

Dear Comrades Kosygin, Gromyko and Distinguished
  Members of the Presidium,
Or whatever you may term yourselves in the current
  Kremlin idiom,
I dismiss as balderdash most of your parroted propa-
  ganda and boorish effrontery,
But I fully agree with your charge that America is the
  foremost Capitalist Country.
This is a point I will not shilly-shally at,
I not only admit, I boast that America has more capi-
  tals than you can shake a Rand McNally at.
Russia has only one capital, Moscow, just as Kenya
  has only one, Nairobi,
But we have Kewanee, Ill., the Pork Chop Capital of
  the World, and Cambridge, Md., the Marsh Rabbit
  Capital of the World, not to mention the Speckled
  Perch Capital of the World, Okeechobee.
Look at Schaller, Iowa, the Popcorn Capital of the
  World, and Washington, Mo., the Corncob Pipe
  Capital of the World, also at the Chitlin Capital
  of the World, a town in South Carolina name of
  Salley,
Yes, and Mansura, La., the Cochon de Lait, or Suck-
  ling Pig, Capital of the World, a capital which is
  right up my gastronomic alley.

Both Berryville, Ark., and Worthington, Minn., claim to be the Turkey Capital of the World and you'd think that Oxboro, Neb., would be as envious as Casca,

But it isn't, it just lays modest claim to being the Turkey Capital of Nebraska.

The Kolach Capital of the World is also in Nebraska, a place called Verdigre,

Although what kolach is I couldn't tell you even under an OGPU third degree.

Hawesville, Ky., is the Sorghum Capital of the World and the Red Flannel Capital of the World is Cedar Springs, Mich.,

And you might like to know that Portland, Oregon, though not a capital, is the Elephant Maternity Ward of the Nation, handy information should your elephant be in a delicate condish.

Rome for a while was the Arsenic Capital of the World in the days of Lucrezia Borgia,

But I'm proud to state that the Collard Seed Capital of the World is our own Cairo, Georgia.

You must confess, Comrades, I have proved it by actual test:

America is not only capital-ist, it is the capital-*est*.

THREE LITTLE MAIDS
FROM SCHOOL

Here is the curious history of three adventurous ladies,
  each of whom was named Françoise.
They all had mastered the art of mistress-ship under
  the tutelage of their ambitious mammas.
They showed themselves eager students,
And at an early age could distinguish prudishness
  from prudence.
Like heliotropes their faces turned towards the Sun
  King, Louis Quatorze,
Who they thought was entitled to a little relaxation
  between wars.
First to feel the glow was Françoise Louise de la
  Baume Le Blanc, Duchesse de la Vallière.
She relaxed Louis to the extent of four children, none
  of whom got to be his heir,
And after the appearance at court of Françoise Athé-
  naïs Rochechouart, Marquise de Montespan, Louis
  did not give her a fifth look,
So she retired to a convent and wrote a religious book.
Then Françoise de Montespan relaxed Louis to the
  extent of several more children, but unwisely en-
  trusted their education to Françoise d'Aubigné,
  Marquise de Maintenon, formerly the impoverished
  widow Scarron,

For whom unwittingly she thus drew from the fire
   the jackpot *marrons,*
Because Françoise de Maintenon became queen and
   Françoise de Montespan retired to a convent which
   she herself had foresightedly founded,
And she didn't write a book but she started a rumor
   which proved that she could still fight even though
   permanently grounded.
There may have been some truth in it, but I myself
   think she went a bit too far;
She whispered that Mme. de Maintenon owed her
   success to the fact that her real name was Mme.
   de Pas-Maintenant-Louis-Mais-Plus-Tard.

WE HAVE MET
THE SASSENACHS
AND THEY ARE OURS;
EVEN THE YEAR
IS NOW McMLXIX

Lang syne 'twas only a pair of Mc's
Gaed wimplin' through the town —
Marshall McLuhan and Rod McKuen,
Wi' never an Alec McCowen.

McLuhan shared a braw pint-stowp
Wi' ghaist or deil or Ouija,
Till himsel' nor naebody else could tell
The messages from the meja.

McKuen trolled the guid folk song
Like "Relique of Bishop Percy,"
And frae dine to ilka mornin' sun
Set the bairns all arsy-versy.

But a' things canty maun come in threes
(Sing thistle, heather, and rowan!);
Quo' Rod McKuen to Marshall McLuhan,
"Ca' oot for Alec McCowen!"

"And gie's a hand, my trusty fiere,"
Says McLuhan to McKuen.

"We'll take a right guid   willie-waught
In honor of the new one."

Now there's three hae rin about the braes
And pu'd fu' monie a gowan —
Marshall McLuhan and Rod McKuen
And His Holiness Alec McCowen.

WHAT DO YOU WANT,
A MEANINGFUL DIALOGUE,
OR A SATISFACTORY TALK?

Bad money drives out good.

That's Gresham's law, which I have not until recently
understood.

No economist I, to economics I have an incurable
allergy,

But now I understand Gresham's law through obvious
analogy.

Just as bad money drives the good beyond our reach,

So has the jargon of the hippie, the huckster and the
bureaucrat debased the sterling of our once lucid
speech.

What's worse, it has induced the amnesia by which
I am faced;

I can't recall the original phraseology which the jar-
gon has replaced.

Would that I had the memory of a computer or an
elephant!

What used I to say instead of uptight, clout and
thrust and relevant?

Linguistics becomes an ever eerier area, like I feel
like I'm in Oz,

Just trying to tell it like it was.

[118]

WHAT'S IT LIKE OUTSIDE?
OR, IT'S ALWAYS FAIR WEATHER UNLESS
SOMEBODY SAYS IT ISN'T

Once there was a man to protect whose reputation I
    shall speak of simply as Horatio.
He believed that weather was created by the latest
    radio report or the Today Show.
For the mad meteorologists of the air he was the ideal
    guinea pig;
He could observe the current weather through his
    window, but he ignored it for news of the approach-
    ing Bermuda high or the Arctic air mass over Medi-
    cine Hat or Winnipeg.
The evidence of his own eyes could not counteract
    his one personal idiosyncrasy,
Which we may well term an audio-videosyncrasy.
For him a rainy day was not rainy nor a sunny day
    sunny unless so certified by his Zenith and his
    Motorola;
He wanted his information straight from the horse's
    mouth, which is to say from the mouth of a Gordon
    Barnes or a Dr. Frank Field or even a Joe Garagiola.
He was cut to the modern pattern;
He took no delight from red sky at night nor warning
    from red sky at morning, and cared not if the moon
    had as many rings as Saturn.

No such old wives' tales for Horatio; old wives' tales were for Arnold Bennett.

Weather is what the radio and the TV say it will be — that was his primary tenet.

Yes, Horatio was, as I have said, a typical product of the audio-video period.

Eventually an April blizzard caught him in shorts and a madras jacket on a day which the Voices assured him was to be fair and warm, and he perished from getting himself thoroughly chilled, virused, and bacteria'd.

WHICH THE CHICKEN,
WHICH THE EGG?

He drinks because she scolds, he thinks;
She thinks she scolds because he drinks,
And neither will admit what's true,
That he's a sot and she's a shrew.

WHO, SIR? ME, SIR? NO, SIR, THE "TIMES," SIR!

> The Marquesa de Portago was married here yesterday afternoon to Richard C. Pistell, the conglomerateur, a one-time merchant seaman who has become the head of a multimillion-dollar industrial empire.
> — *New York Times*

In a song of my youth the singer sang of the sunshine
   in the eyes of his beloved and the roses in her
   cheeks, which when they met, presumably in the
   vicinity of her nose,
They represented to him the wedding of the sunshine
   and the rose.
That wedding has clung to my memory like a burr,
And now I have a new memory-clinger, one recently
   chronicled by the *Times*, the mystic union between
   a Marquesa and a conglomerateur.
The *Times* didn't state whether he was an amateur
   conglomerateur or a pro,
But since it referred to him as the head of a multi-
   million-dollar industrial empire I assume that the
   latter is so.
I hope that in his happiness he will not be alone,
I hope that every oilateur and shipping magnateur

and scrap-metalateur, indeed every tycoonateur, will
   soon have a Marquesa of their own.
I think that once they have the climax capped they
   should adorn and bedizen it;
After all, to eur is human, isn' it?

YOU STEER AND I'LL TOOT,
OR, ALL'S SLICK THAT ENDS SLICK

Henry Henley had a hero, Henry the Navigator, that
  maritime-minded Portuguese prince,
Whom he wished to be the greatest navigator since.
Perhaps from this decision he might have divagated
Had he known, as you and I know, that Henry the
Navigator never navigated.
Not only had he never navigated, he never even made
  a voyage.
He just had a lot of navigators in his employage.
Of the truth I am not an extravagator
When I reckon that had he ever tried to navigate he
  would not have been called Henry the Navigator.
Thus it is obvious that if Henry wished to earn that
  sobriquet it was foolish of him to want to navigate;
He had no more sense of direction than a crab, or
  indeed a crab ravigote.
None could deny his pluck,
But while yet a babe in the bath he couldn't correct
  the course of a yawing celluloid duck.
As a courting swain on the lake in Central Park he
  attempted simultaneously to row and woo,
Thereby achieving temporary fame as the only adult
  unaccompanied by a child to ground his boat in
  the Children's Zoo.

The day he was appointed to the Steering Committee
of his boat club his heart was light as a perfect
chicken vol-au-vent,
But after a year of Henry's steering the club was hope-
lessly insolovent.
You might suppose that at this point he would have
ceased to dream of being known as Henry the
Navigator II and quietly dropped anchor,
But he didn't, and he is now captain of a spanking
new 70,000-ton tanker.

YOU COULD KNOCK SOME
PEOPLE OVER WITH
A FEATHER,
OR, LIFE IS JUST A BOWL OF SURPRISES

"And in this hotel the hot water faucet was on the
    right and the cold water faucet on the left, did you
    ever hear of such a thing in your life?"
Thus spake Mr. Bodfish's dinner partner, whose con-
    versation with this interrogatory challenge was rife.
Mr. Bodfish said he might have, yes, he recalled a
    hotel adventure that befell a distant cousin in Sep-
    tember, no, October of '55 or it may have been '56;
Be that as it may, the place was Rome, and she sud-
    denly found herself in an exasperating fix.
She was perfecting a spitcurl when she looked down
    and wished that she had a musket or a broom or a
    scimitar,
Because what do you think, a mouse was skirting her
    peignoir's perimeter.
Lacking weapons, she immediately telephoned the
    floor waiter, and to expedite matters spoke in Italian
    and asked for a *gatto,* or cat,
And her order came up in nothing flat,
But there was an awkward mistake,
Because the waiter was not Italian, he was French,
    and he brought her a *gâteau,* or cake.

She was upbraiding the luckless lackey when he was
interceded for by the mouse, who had hitherto
hesitated to speak;
He allowed as he'd rather have a cake than a cat any
day in the week.
Mr. Bodfish awaited with interest the result of this
provocative endeavor,
And he was not surprised when first the lady asked,
Did you ever? then without pause for reflection
gave her decision, Well, I never!